EJPublishers

Bird Guy

Wally Karr's Poems about Birds

Grade Nine English Project

Yours in writing,
David Booth

David Booth

Dedication:
To the students in
Queen Mary and Dalewood Schools
all those years ago,
and to the Jay that flew into my life.

Text copyright © 2018 by the publisher:
Elizabeth James Publishers
Toronto, Canada

ElizabethJamesPublishers@gmail.com

E|Publishers

Illustrator: Maya Ishiura
Cover: Lisa Juan
Editor: Bryan Wright

Printed by Createspace
ISBN 9781717173041

Available from Amazon.com
and other book stores

TABLE OF CONTENTS

Introducing the Project

The First Monday

It all began with Mr. Moore's introduction
to the year-long project:

Memo to Ninth-Grade Students:
This is the beginning of your year-long
English writing project. I will work
with each of you on a pilot study.
This will set the conditions for your own work,
once I have approved it.

Mr. Moore then interviewed me
about my idea for writing poems about birds.
He said, as a pilot project to begin my study,
that I should choose a bird I have seen
on my nature walks, describe my bird,
and include an illustration.

The Next Monday:

School projects- why I hate school.
No one to help me, can't tell my family or they will try,
and I put projects off until the last moment.
Everyone else has begun their project.
I have a whole year of pain ahead of me.
What will I do?

The Monday after That

I drop by the library after four
and ask her for a bird book.
She says, "Haven't chosen your project yet,
have you." I reply, "Yes I have,
but I need more information for my report."
She says, "Oh."
And there it is on the counter:
The Audubon Book of Birds.
I flip through.
I see a picture of an olive-green bird.
You won't believe it,
but I have an olive-green pencil crayon
in my pencil case.
This was meant to be.

Ovenbirds are olive-green above and spotted below, with bold black-and-orange crown stripes. A white eye ring gives it a somewhat surprised expression. Like several other terrestrial, or near-terrestrial, warblers, Ovenbirds have pink legs. They have been seen in Southern Ontario.

I copy the information on my iPad.
I am at last ready for the final project. Wait.
I didn't actually see an ovenbird.
But I did see the picture in the book.

And they say a picture is worth
a thousand words.
If I am careful, I will just mention
how I spotted the bird among the leaves.
(Book leaves.)

I am done.
The project finished.
The illustration perfect.
The green a subtle olive.
The bird described in detail, in full.
I am handing the work in to be marked.
I am not nervous.
Maybe a bit.

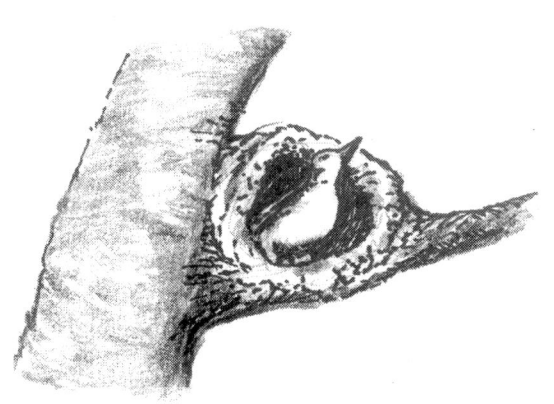

The Next Monday:

He is handing the projects back today.
I am next.
I take the project, glance at the mark:
$\mathcal{A}$-.
I read the comments:

Well-written. Good drawing. Unusual bird.
Fortunate that you saw it in its natural habitat.
What a lucky coincidence that
you had an olive-green pencil crayon.
The same shade as used by Mr. Audubon.
I will add your ovenbird to your project.
You have a year. Good luck.
A year among the birds.

W. H. Moore

The bell rings.

I avoid his eyes as I leave the room.

Still my favorite teacher.

FAMILIAR FEATHERS

I am actually a pretty honest kid.
I wanted to do a good job on this project.
I respect Mr. Moore. He makes English come alive.
And he approved my idea for observing and writing poems
about birds.
I shouldn't have explained my writing project to the class.
Norm called out, "Hey Bird Guy!", and it stuck.
But Mara sits next to me in class.
She likes the ideas of writing poems.
She is researching strange inventions
inside the Harry Potter books: could they actually
be constructed?
I am sticking to birds.
My grandparents have bird feeders in their garden.
My dad is a writer. That is my family,
and now you understand the reason for my project.
I have a month to finish the first section of my report.
I am going to begin with the birds I can find easily,
not that I am lazy,
but I have to research the information as well.
Autumn birds.
I will begin with them.
There is a bird on the window ledge
outside our classroom.
Is that lucky or not?

Two Faces

There is a pigeon on the sill.
The sill ten stories high.
Why is the pigeon here at all,
Forgotten how to fly?

Is this bird just halfway home
And found a resting place?
Will he spend the evening here
Or fly off into space?

We own different solitudes,
The window shut forever.
The pigeon sitting on the sill,
Brief shelter from the weather.

Stay here as long as needed,
the window sill is free.
As darkness falls, I see my face
in glass reflecting me.

But you remain outside my life,
A moment face to face.
I will leave, and you will leave,
With just a memory trace.

City Songs

Sitting in my living room twenty stories high
at 7:30 in the morning, the sounds of birds
fill the air. Chirps, whistles, cheeps and trills
and the occasional twitter, they pull me
to the window and on to the balcony
that is forbidden to me unless my dad
is present. But I am driven to slide open
the patio door, to seek out the talkers
and the squawkers and the singers
and the warblers hidden by the leaves
in the few trees that survive the city asphalt
and cement. "Where are you?" I cry out.
I want to applaud our city orchestra.
I want to conduct the next overture.
I am with them, silent, but with them.
I will be your road crew, your manager.
Let me fly with you. I will work for free!
And just then the bus roars into my concert,
and, as if by one signal from the lead guitarist,
the birds are gone. I turn and go inside,
pick up my backpack, put in my earbuds,
and begin the trek to school.

Trees or Birds?

Emily Carr painted trees.
Huge, trunks climbing skyward,
seeking the sounds of lumberjacks
to warn the others.
I can almost hear the growing pains
of the branches.
Are the birds hidden
in the dark, unrelenting colours?
Did Emily Carr not see them,
not notice the birds for the trees?
I will only paint the birds.
The trees are resting places.
They are hers.
The birds are mine.

Red Warning

Red-winged blackbird,
who paints your wings?
A slash of colour startling us.
We see you in those bushes, hiding.
Your marking makes you obvious.
But should you want to disappear,
Your wings will always cause you grief,
Undone by such a neon signal —
A glimpse of red, however brief.

Hangers-on

The nuthatches have arrived
this morning.
Shouting out their wake-up calls,
they gather on the bird feeder,
tiny, soft creatures who know
some survival tricks, hanging
upside down, head first —
feathered acrobats
fleeing from Cirque du Soleil.
And they carry those large
sunflower seeds to a tiny crevice
in the bark of the nearby birch,
wedge them in, and
with their strong little beaks,
crack them open, true to their name.
They own the bird feeder this morning,
territorial diners who wish no company
as they mine the rich resource
hanging from the slippery steel pole
that is the bane of those without wings,
without tricks.

Bird is Word

Hawk is eye,
Owl is stare,
Robin — spring,
Dove is pair.
Vulture — death,
Albatross — fear,
Crow is thief,
Seagull — pier.
Loon is laugh,
Cardinal — red,
Jay is blue,
Pigeon — bread.
Swan is glide,
Crane is leg,
Sparrow — flock,
Chicken — egg.
Turkey — farm,
Wren is small,
Hummingbird — wings,
Ostrich — tall.
For each bird,
Just one word,
One feathered thought —
The bird is heard.

Crossing the Heavens

I saw them before I heard them.
Eyes toward heaven, the V signal
growing larger as they approached,
unaware of all below, sky bound,
each bird flying slightly above
the bird in front, defeating the resistance
of the Wind God.

Not afraid as fatigue strikes to draw back
from the front, taking turns as leaders,
every bird aware of the other,
gliding when they can, wings beating
when needed, synergy and energy,
the icons of flight. "I am here with you!"
the geese honk again and again.

Together is better.
And when one falters
and falls to earth, the flock lands
beside the injured and guards
and protects the one
until recovery or loss.
Then, lift off, and in moments,
the perfect V shape heading towards
the ancient yet known destination.
The earth clock finds its seasons
through these geese flights,
heralding spring and exiting winter,
crossing the heavens, as they should.

Winter is coming in late autumn,
and the birds are always on time.

Birds in Hard Hats

The staccato sounds reverberate
through the trees
surrounding the lake-view cottage.
The workers have begun early today —
hammering, drilling, boring,
excavating, tapping,
with red work hats protecting their skulls,
thick bristles protecting their nostrils
from flying wood chips,
a chisel and crowbar called beaks
to remove bark and locate bugs,
and a tongue-catcher four inches long
with glue on the tip for extracting insects
who are hidden deep,
tail feathers stiff enough to support
the force pounding the bodies,
drilling 10,000 times a day, every day,
feet protected by two sharply-clawed
lumberjack toes pointing in each direction,
digging into the sides of the trees
as the worker balances and drills.

Woodpeckers — nature's jackhammers,
hiding acorns in holes for lunchtime,
when there may be moments
for a few gentle love-taps
on the tree trunk, signalling for a female
to drop in, a coded text message
that makes the worker's day fly by.

All in Together

The song says,
"His eye is on the sparrow,
and I know he watches me."

A flock of them is on my front lawn.
Unafraid of me or perhaps anything,
except cats.
Bobbing around, searching
for tiny insects,
living la vida loca.
One eats from my hand, Rice Krispies.
One grain at a time.

So many sparrows, all over the world,
some smaller, some greyer,
all sparrows.

His eye, they say, is on all of them.
If everyone matters, then so must I.

Sparrows and me,
on the front lawn.

Sparrow

Owl Trouble

Crows detest you.
With its sharp eyes, one spots you,
lets out a 'caw'
that tells the others you are here.
Gathering around you,
perching as close as possible,
cawing at the top of their ragged voices,
tormenting until you can stand it
no longer, you fly off with a scream,
followed by this noisy feathered mob,
this tail of tormentors.
Owl, you frighten me.
Owl, you fascinate me.

Owl Questions

Why do you hoot, Owl?
What do you see?
What do you want, Owl,
Up in your tree?

What do you spy, Owl,
Far down below?
Turning your head, Owl,
What do you know?

Why hunt at night, Owl?
Moon's in the sky.
Daybreak will come, Owl,
Where will you fly?

Where is your child, Owl?
I see the dawn!
Why are you sad, Owl?
Owlet has gone.

Parking Spaces

Why is that seagull sitting
in a parking space
in this car lot?
What is it waiting for?
Seems to be confident
that something good
is about to happen.
Always does, I guess.

But who will come along
with something worth eating?
There isn't a single car
parked here. An empty lot.
Seagull pecks at a crack
in the asphalt. Nothing there.
A sauna? Is the dark heat
relaxing seagull's muscles?
Is life in a parking lot life?
I guess.

So little expectation
frees you from the torture chamber
of the struggle for success.
Let the other birds
fight over a hamburger bun
in the empty lot next door.

Seagull will take his chances
on future happenings right here.
Taking life as it comes.
One crumb at a time.

Look! An ant. Gone.
Seagull can't smile,
but who cares?
One ant at a time.

Great Blue Heron

I cannot walk on stilts
But you can.
Standing motionless,
So patient
In the shallow water,
Until a fish or a frog
Passes by.
A quick thrust of your long neck,
A stab of your spear-bill
Leaves you silently
Alone.

STRANGE FEATHERS

Each bird looks different.
From age to age, from season to season,
from place to place.
Birds' bodies change.
Only birders recognize
the many stages of life,
just as humans grow older, greyer, smaller.
The rest of us simply see the bird we first knew.
A starling is a starling, a finch a finch.
We, of course, have favorites in the feathered world,
but some seem outside our frame of reference.
Strange creatures, relegated to other imaginations, unfamiliar,
even disturbing.
Some of us wonder about these nervous of creatures
who can fly away at any second,
who can exist on bugs and berries,
who can stare at us from treetops.
So many species of birds,
just one for humans, I guess.
Do they follow us with their sharp eyes,
laughing at our actions,
wondering about our behaviors?
Do they care who we are?
They sing when they feel like it.
I wish I could.

Seven Bird Dreams

Do birds dream?

Of cats being sent to islands
without trees
so that birds can have safe landing
on the mainland?

Of squirrels, suddenly sickened
by bird food and refusing to climb
the poles holding feeders
for our winter feathered friends?

Of scarecrows who suddenly
wave their gloves
welcoming the birds,
asking them to feast
on the fields of seeds?
The farmers
have more than enough anyway.

Of hot baked pies
full of four and twenty
of some other species –
maybe human?

Of pecking on the outside
of a cage containing
a human specimen,
and whistling happy tunes
while checking to make certain
the cage door is fastened?

Of a wizard that tells his secret
for filling the net
with slippery fish forever?

Of knowing that their eggs
of every colour would
remain untouched
except for the mother, until
cracking out of all the shells,
the babies breathe
that blue and deep air?

Boxer Birds

I was just standing there minding
my own business, when an explosion
filled the sky above my head
and a blur of orange and blue
fell at my feet.
I stared at a clump of feathers,
and saw that an oriole and a blue jay
had somehow become tangled in the sky.
They had lost control of gravity, and
ended up on the ground right beside me.
I couldn't move. I mean, even when I realized
what had happened.
Should I lift them apart and bury them
in my garden, or should I ...
But the remains stirred,
and two embarrassed creatures with wings
lifted off, leaving me alone on earth.
I stared as their paths parted
and each flew to safety.
I am sure that this will never happen again
but every time I enter into my aunt's garden
my eyes are pulled upward
in search of an orange and blue tornado.
If only they had left me a souvenir,
two feathers, one orange, one blue,
I would have kept them in my wallet,
beside the picture of my mother,
another memory.

A Murder of Crows

Such an apt descriptor.
Sitting on the sky wires,
Waiting.
For a signal?
For a sign?
All of the crows silent,
Screams held for the moment.
Do they sense death?
Of an unfortunate crow?
Road kill?
A body?
Are they watching me?
I am innocent!
I am walking away.
The crows stare,
Still silent.
Feathered undertakers
Dressed for the event.
Prepared.
Always.

The Bullied

Seven huge ravens
Roost in that tree.
Sharp-beaked birds,
Staring at me.

I sit on this bench
Every day.
Afraid to move,
On display.

Am I waiting for them?
Are they waiting for me?
Break the spell,
Set us free.

But no one does
And the birds appear.
I close my eyes
And live in fear.

Atlas and the World

I was standing
in the rain
holding up a large, black umbrella
(the kind you see in ads),
and I felt something land
on my rain-proof tent
and then something else,
and another.
Not wanting to put the umbrella down
and get wet,
I carefully turned around
and saw my reflection in a store window
(I noticed it sold umbrellas,
large black ones.)

There, sitting on mine, were three big birds
not caring about the rain.

I couldn't shake them free.
(I don't know why.)
I was Atlas holding
up their world.
I didn't want to force them
to fly into the storm.

My bus was coming,
And I knew the moment was near.

I would like to say
that suddenly,
with their claws,
they picked up the umbrella and me,
and carried me home,
dropping me carefully on
the front walk.
However, that would be
someone else's life,
a comic strip.
I had to board the bus
to reach my home.
And looking up
at the underside of my umbrella,
Atlas shrugged,
and the birds flew off.

Is That a Budgie?

There are budgies in the woods.
Shots of pink and green and mauve
and yellow surprising my eyes. Why?
Why in the woods, not in a cage?
Do woods folk keep budgie birds
in their cabins? Or did these pieces
of brilliant flashes plan a mass escape
from comfy sitting rooms
with easy chairs covered in bird prints,
and using the magnetic forces
flee to this wild hinterland?
Not only that, I saw a poodle running
with a pack of dogs, or coyotes, or wolves.
A poodle with its tail clipped.
Am I too tied up in what should be?
A bird is a bird is a bird, wherever.
But a poodle? Can it survive?
I am sitting in the back seat
of my dad's '63 Falcon
flying down the highway,
trees on either side.
Rural — urban. Who is what?
My goldfish lives in a bowl.
Why?

Night Lights

Relax. I knew they weren't birds.
Even when I was six. They fly, though.
They have wings. Fireflies, of course.
At first, I thought they were just sparks
as I stared from my bedroom window.
After all, it was fireworks night
and the sounds and colours filled
the evening. Do these creatures think
that the gun powder splotches
are distant relatives they don't want to know?
When I went downstairs into the back yard,
I saw the flickering insects everywhere.
And then I remembered the glass jars
from my sixth birthday, when I caught ten
and caged them in their invisible prison.
Nothing remained the next morning
but bits of bug on the bottom of the jar.
This time, I let the pinpoints of light
continue to give their warning signals,
or show their joy at just being in the soft night
when the jar-keepers are all asleep.
I will not try to own these red dots;
they are free to come and go,
to shine on whenever they feel like it.
Six-year-olds don't understand
these mysteries of nature as I do.
Now I can turn my own light on and off,
on, off, on, off, only when I decide.

The Fixer-Upper

June 1st.
I hear a rustling in the bushes
along the driveway.
A squirrel? A snake?

Actually, a crow.
Not large, black, its eye
spotting me. I am motionless.
It continued its task,
pulling at the dried strands
of stems at the base
of the plant's spear-like leaves.
Even dead, the straw leaves
clung to the root base as the crow
pulled at one of them, again
and again, until it gave way.

Holding it in its beak,
the crow found another one,
even larger, and the struggle
began again. A small victory
with two strands in its beak,
like a yellow moustache.

Crows are seldom quitters:
more attacks at this harvest
until the gleaner held
what to the crow was
a bale of straw in its beak.

The task completed,
the crow left land so quickly,
flew straight toward the only tree
on the street, and I guess,
continued to renovate the nest,
in time for the children to arrive.

This crow could star
in a *Fix Up Your Home* show on cable.
I would watch it for sure.

FAMILY FEATHERS

I wasn't sure about
the memoir part of this project.
I mean, it's about birds, not me.
But then, I began thinking of my family-
dad, grandparents, cousins, neighbours, friends,
and I realized that
birds of a feather flock together,
as the saying goes. So I began to notice
the birds around our home,
in our relatives' lives, next door,
on our holidays, and a flock of ideas
came to me.

I hope that the kids in my class
start to notice their own lives,
begin to observe as social scientists,
and record their information and feelings.
I spend so much time
revising my poems,
but it is like playing hockey:
you want to learn more,
to move up a level.
I never feel a poem is finished.
I never score a goal.
I just enjoy the game.

Pigeons and Popcorn

I am feeding the pigeons
in Trafalgar Square.
Popcorn.
I am standing beside the statue
of Lord Nelson.
I am not moving.
The pigeons are resting on my head,
on my outstretched arms.
Others are flapping around me
or eating popcorn from around my feet.
I am one with the birds.
Bird Guy.

My dad is taking pictures of me
and the birds.
I don't know why.
Maybe to show at my wedding
in twenty years.
And what will people think?
"What a crazy kid."
"Don't birds spread disease?"

Just then a London cop
clapped his hands and the birds disappeared.
He told my dad that this event
was no longer allowed,
and we were lucky
he wasn't giving us a summons.

We left and went
to a KFC restaurant.
In London, England, a KFC.
We had fried chicken,
checked out the pictures
of the pigeons and me,
and laughed.
"Doesn't that tickle
your funny bone?" he said.
"When that cop appeared,
you could have knocked me over
with a feather."
I answered," A pigeon feather."
He laughed.
"Birds of a feather, we are."
"You and me."
I will keep the picture forever.

My Cousins Keep Pigeons, Too

More than a million homing pigeons die every year during Taiwan's seasonal pigeon races, grueling sets of seven races over open ocean from ever-increasing distances. Young birds— not even a year old— are shipped out to sea, released in the middle of the ocean and forced to fly back home even in the midst of typhoon-strength winds. Most often, less than 1 percent of these highly intelligent birds complete each seven-race series; many drown from exhaustion, perish in the storms, or are killed afterward for being too slow.

Norm and Ed are brothers.
They keep pigeons in the garage.
Homing pigeons
of every colour you could imagine.
Their dad parks his car on the street,
the joy of living in a small town.
Ed, the elder, owns thirty birds.
Norm, the younger, owns twenty birds.
Every Sunday, unless they were playing
in the marching band,
Ed, the trumpet,
Norm, the bugle,
the boys open the garage doors
to the sounds of fifty birds shouting at them.
Each boy selects five birds,
places five in each wicker basket,
walks to the open garage door,

and lifts the baskets into the trunk of the car.
Ed, the senior, will drive.
He is sixteen and has a licence.
Norm and I jump in.
We make a U-turn and head east.
The sun is rising and causes a glaring screen
on the smudged front window of the car.
No one can hear the birds.
We arrive at the old movie drive-in
at the edge of town. The screen has been
empty for years. The sign from the last film
still says "The Birds" by Alfred Hitchcock.
Ed and Norm get out and open the trunk,
lifting the baskets onto an old picnic table.
They open the lids, carefully lift each bird out,
and toss them, one by one, into the air.
The creatures twirl and flutter,
gradually form a flock, and head west.
Ed and Norm return to the car
where I am waiting, drive off, heading west
as well. They arrive home in twenty-minutes,
and on the garage roof, waiting,
are ten pigeons, cooing.
Norm says, "They made it."
Ed says, "Of course."
Cousins are great. They trust pigeons. And me.

Counting Feathers

My grandfather is sitting in the tree
in our backyard.
He has nailed boards to the trunk
as a make-shift ladder.
He won't descend until he has seen
his quota for the day.
He writes in his bird journal
with a fountain pen filled
with green ink, from a lifetime supply
in his desk drawer.
His Peterson Bird Guide
is almost worn through.
I think he has seen every bird
mentioned in the book.
Since he retired from his job
as a school bus driver,
he says that the birds have become
his children.
By being among them, and
by noticing their arrivals and
leave-takings, their feathery world
somehow matters more.
I watch him from my bedroom window.
He sits on a small platform he has built
in the V of the trunk,
and observes, noting each bird he sees
in his journal, with green ink.

When his mission is complete
for the day, he will come
into the kitchen and
call me down from my room
to share one or two
of his remarkable observations.
This week:
American Woodcock
Northern Saw-whet Owl
Ruby-throated Hummingbird
Northern Flicker
Red-breasted Nuthatch
Golden-crowned Kinglet
Canada Warbler
Rose-breasted Grosbeak
White-throated Sparrow
Northern Oriole.
He reads each entry aloud to me
as we drink our tea.
His bird book with yellow pages,
green ink.
My grandfather and me.
Feather words.

The Bridge

I never stay up until midnight.
Not allowed.
Except once in Denmark
When there was no night
Only day in that northern world.
And I am walking home
With my family, across a bridge
That leads to our hotel
When we hear
The flapping of wings
And looking down
From the walled side
We see a flock of swans
Flying under the bridge
That we are standing on.
The sky was bright,
The water black,
The swans grey.
We stared until
They were swallowed
By the horizon.
Hans Christian Andersen
Had called them home
To rest inside his tales.

Loon's Call

The drive to the cottage takes three hours
of traffic fumes, cramped quarters,
sibling arguments,
with chopped egg sandwiches
and juice boxes to give us strength
for the journey every Friday night,
as my father listens to the CBC news
and we, saved by earbuds and rock,
beat time with our fingers and arrive
at dusk and while we unpack we hear it
and no one moves because the loon
owns the night and the lake and our hearts
and we are grateful for the smell of pine,
the white of birch, the feel of sand,
but especially for the sound of loon,
the cottage landlord.

I Live in a Birdhouse

When I was five years old,
my uncle helped me to build a birdhouse.
We worked in his garage with saws and wood
and tools from his tool box. Bright red.
I thought he was a genius.
He let me saw the wood for the roof,
and drill a hole for the birds to come and go.
We painted the birdhouse yellow
with a red roof.

It took a week for the birdhouse
to dry. Then my uncle came to my house
and I helped him nail the birdhouse
to the pole in our backyard.
That birdhouse is still there.
I can see it from my bedroom window.
My uncle is gone now.
Eight years have passed.
But there are no birds
in that wooded home.
Never were. Didn't matter.
My uncle knew that I was the bird.
He made me a home. I still live inside
the bird house. I am five years old again.

The Birds on My Uncle's Head

I mean, who could take him seriously,
with two birds sitting on his head.
Yes, they were pets — parakeets —
but how was I to have a discussion
with this weird sight staring me in the eye.
I mean, if he were feeding pigeons in the park
I would snap a picture and laugh later.
But I am to have a difficult conversation
that will need eye contact
and careful answers to difficult questions.
And those birds keep staring at me,
shifting position,
and my uncle sees nothing unusual
about the whole situation.
Oh, I managed, don't ask me how.
I went home afterwards
with his feathered hat
still in front of my eyes.

Two days later, a cat did away
with my uncle's pet birds.
He had them in a golden cage on the patio.
I had called him about those questions,
and when he went inside
to answer the phone, the deed was done.
The birds are no longer there.
I wish they were.

Three Geese

The geese are always flying
towards the hallway
in my aunts' kitchens.
Three geese:
the big one, the middle one, the small one,
flying nowhere, living their lives in kitchens,
frozen in midair, nailed to the wall.

Three aunts:
the young one, the middle one, the older one,
all with three geese,
like in some strange fairy tale.
Are they taught this as girls?
"Get the geese as soon as you are married!"
Where do you buy these geese?

Three kitchens:
One wall — sky blue. That makes sense.
One wall — tomato red. Why?
One wall — bright yellow. Into the sun.
Three aunts, three geese, three walls.

Harbingers of hope,
freedom from the daily drudge?
Will these aunts one day fly away?
Will they take these geese with them?
Do my uncles notice the geese?
Do they notice my aunts?

Is it a ritual —
geese on the kitchen wall,
a painting above the couch,
a kid's drawing on the fridge,
running shoes piled in the hallway?
I know it's strange but I love the geese.
We don't have any on our wall.
If I had a mother, I guess we would.
     I guess.

CANADA GEESE

Growing Wings

My cousin Michael said he could feel them
just beneath his shoulders.
But children of sixteen
are always growing and
knowing all there is to know.
And I pooh-poohed
his mentioning something about
his body changing
at this time of life.

Did I hear him telling
a friend on the phone
the other evening?
Teenagers and their worries.

It happened when I was away
at camp for two weeks.
When I arrived home,
my father said my cousin
was flying around somewhere.
I knew what he meant.

My grandmother had told me a story
years ago and only now did it make sense.
I ran outside, shaded my eyes
and looked up.
I saw a speck against the clouds.
The speck was my cousin.
Flying free.

There was nothing to say,
even if I could have found words.

An hour later he came back
and I offered him some Nachos
and an orange drink
in the back yard near the bird bath.

Now he covers his wings
while in the house,
under jackets with rock star faces
or T-shirts with sports teams.
But the wings are still there.

And when he calls
"I'm going out for a while,"
I know where.
I no longer scan the skies.
After all, bird boys need freedom.
Life will soon clip their wings.

I am looking in the mirror,
holding another mirror in my hand,
checking my back.
Nothing. No wings.

Chickadee Sunday

They are outside the kitchen window
feasting on the bird seeds my grandmother
has tossed on the fallen snow —
peanuts, milo, white millet, sunflower.
She does this once a week.
On chickadee Sunday.

The birds eat together:
reservations for twelve for dinner.
It is -10 degrees Celsius. No bother.

Appropriate dress:
black caps; thick feathers they lift
to trap warm air to insulate against the cold,
their own down-filled comforters.

No appetizers for chickadee diners.
They eat constantly —
chickadee cuisine: insect eggs, lice, weevils,
but today —
gourmet seeds. Thanks to the chef
staring out the window.

Our cat sits on the table beside us.
Staring at feathers.
No hawk circles above their heads.
The deal is dinner in safety.
We guarantee it.

The feathered performance is finished.
No dessert.
On a secret signal, there is lift-off.
The snow is hardly disturbed.
Feather-brushed a little.
Two seeds remain. Leftovers.
Grandma kisses the top of my head.
I smile.

Chickadee

Real or Fake?

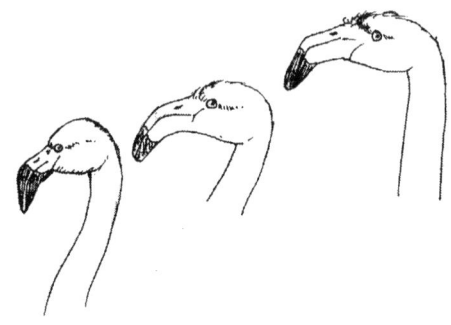

So we are in Florida, and my grandmother
has one wish: to see real flamingos.
She has seven fake ones in her front yard,
a surprise for her 75th birthday.
Seven of them.
"I want to see a real one," she says.
"Are they really pink?"

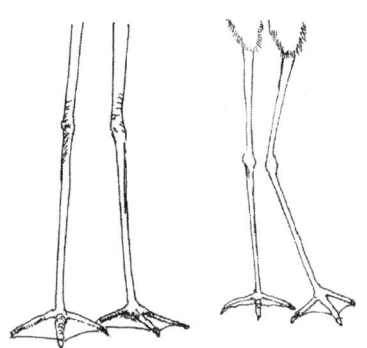

In our four days there,
we have a lot to do:
Disney World, the Epcot Centre,
the ocean, and four shopping malls.
We haven't seen one flamingo.
Until now.

A whole field of flamingos.
A community of these birds.
And they are pink. Bright pink.
"I knew it. I knew it," she said,
"just like the ones on my front yard."
The guide gave us a brochure,
and would you believe it, it says
they are pink and reddish
because they eat
certain algae and invertebrates
that contain beta carotene.
Like carrots and sweet potatoes.

I read once that if you eat
too many carrots
your skin can turn orange.
There's the proof.

Next day, we are waiting
for my grandmother
to come out of the beauty parlor,
when we see her wave to us,
and her hair is pink.
Actually pink.

"If I came all this way to see a flamingo,
I am going home with a real memory."
And it was exactly the same colour
as the birds.
Fake birds and pink hair:
"Real" is in the eye of the beholder.
Pass me a carrot stick.

Feathers and Leaves

My grandmother is surrounded
by feathers. She sleeps
on a feather mattress,
a feather comforter,
a feather pillow,
never remembering the feathers.
They are but a means to an end.

Warmth, a cocoon hiding from the cold.
Her fire, a wood stove in the kitchen.
She, wrapped in a flannel nightgown.
The feathers, invisible, weightless,
covered in cotton washed smooth,
bleached by the sun and clothesline,
then the dried encased feathers
shaken and punched into some semblance
of shape.
The birds have no idea
about their body coverings
being transformed into human comfort.
They are long gone, forgotten, repurposed.
Like the leaves that become mulch
over the tulips, covering the bulbs,
no longer green, simply unknown
tree memories.

Birds and leaves that once swooped
and fluttered,
now protecting bits of life. She, now old
and lighter than smoke,
sleeps on the feather bed below,
her comforter above,
guarded by wings without intent, safe.

Bird Guy

Let me fly with you
Higher, yet higher,
Till clouds are below us
That's all I require.

To leave solid ground,
To be lighter than air,
I just want to fly
Beside you, a pair.

Boy beside bird,
Bird leading boy,
Together we soar,
Highflying joy.

Goodbye to my home,
Bid adieu to my friends,
So long to my family,
My earthly life ends.

One with the birds,
My loneliness gone,
My life changed forever,
My world moving on.

I am now bird,
With no human form,
My arms become wings,
My body reborn.

Goodbye to what was,
We greet the new sky,
My partner a bird,
Together we fly.

We fly. We fly.

TICKLING FEATHERS

At Boy Scouts tonight, I received
my *Bird Study* badge.
I have several badges now,
but I am the only one
with this particular badge.
I studied hard, and did all the activities.
But I also made these tasks
part of my year-long writing project.
I hope that is ethical.
I am worried that my Scoutmaster
played favorites with me,
but he is quite tough about cheating.
And poems aren't part
of the badge requirements,
so I guess that's fair.
Although if there were a badge for poetry,
I would deserve it.
But my Scoutmaster would have to approve it.
Mr. Moore is tough. Oh, yes.
He is my English teacher, too.
I don't know if he will approve
of my humorous poems about birds.
I have never seen him laugh. Except once.
Someone threw a snowball
through the classroom window,
and it hit him on the head. He laughed. We did not.
Then he went on reading the novel to us.
But he did laugh.

Birds of the Week

Swanday
Martinday
Ternday
Wrensday
Thrushday
Finchday
Sapsuckerday

Responsibility

Once, I had to look after
my friend's blue budgie-bird
with a long tail.
The second day, I let it out
of the cage,
and it flew onto the stove
and sat on a pan of
Campbell's Tomato Soup.
Its tail stuck in the soup,
and turned bright red.
My friend came home.

Feathered Fun

Ten little starlings
Sitting on a wire,
One flew off,
Soared a little higher.

Nine little starlings
Sitting on a wire,
One flew off,
Witnessing a fire.

Eight little starlings
Sitting on a wire,
One flew off,
Landing on a spire.

Seven little starlings
Sitting on a wire,
One flew off,
And settled in a briar.

Six little starlings
Sitting on a wire,
One flew off,
He decided to retire.

Five little starlings
Sitting on a wire,
One flew off,
Determined to inquire.

Four little starlings
Sitting on a wire,
One flew off,
Joined a larger choir.

Three little starlings
Sitting on a wire,
One flew off,
Heard the cannon fire.

Two little starlings
Sitting on a wire,
One flew off,
Lost all of her desire.

One little starling
Sitting on a wire,
Stayed where she was.
That I quite admire.

Guano

There the word was
in black and white.
Right in the science text book.
Guano.
We knew the teacher would say,
"Look it up," so we did.
Winston School Dictionary.
It had failed us on all the words
we actually wanted to know about,
but we tried again:
"Manure used as fertilizer in Peru
from sea birds."
Then the teacher came by our desks,
so I said: "What does the word
man-oo-re mean, sir?"
He told us in a loud voice,
"It's pronounced *manure,*
and it means bird or animal poop."
The whole class heard.
Of course they laughed.
Why wouldn't they?
Some words are not meant
to be heard.
Guano is one of them.
Leave it for the birds.

Voted #1

I want to thank all of those
who voted for me
as Canada's national bird,
the emblem of this great country.
Of course, no birds voted.
I am embarrassed
but proud of this honor.
I realize the snowy owl,
the loon and the Canada goose
were runners up, and I wish them
no harm. Of course, you may not know
that we do not migrate, that we are
a truly Canadian species.
Feel free now to call me "Canada Jay,"
or, as the First Peoples say,
"Wisakedjak," or the contemporary slang:
 Whiskey Jack."
I will admit to a strong intelligence.
Some find me mischievous,
as are my cousins, Raven and Crow.
I consider myself tough and adaptable,
and I certainly am not a show-off.
Have you seen me? Probably not.
They chose Loon for the two-dollar coin.
Was I annoyed?
Perhaps. But now, I am Bird of Canada.
That's right: Bird of Canada.
Hee hee hee hee!

Mimic Me

The mockingbird can mimic
all kinds of other birds.
One managed to sound
like 55 species in one hour.
Another sounded like
a squeaky wheelbarrow.
His friend barked like a dog.
One croaked like a frog.
His buddy imitated a car alarm
going on and going off.
Do mocking birds ever forget
who they really are?
Do they end up in a red-wing's nest
by mistake?

Like the mockingbird,
I am not who you think.
I am who I choose to be.
At this moment.
Listen away today;
Tomorrow's sounds will change.
I am what I hear nearby.
I steal a voice or two.
Perhaps borrow is a more apt term.
No one really knows me.
Girls just hear me.
Who am I, Mr. Mockingbird?
Who are you?

The Gulls and the Chip Wagon

There are French fries placed
on a china plate,
and there are chips wrapped
in a newspaper.
Frankly, I'm talking about
the second variety.
Big, fat slices of potato
perfectly cooked.
Only from the chip wagon
under the bridge
to Port Huron.
It has been there all my life.
Whenever I am
in the neighbourhood
I pay a friendly visit
for a full tank fill-up
and I remember that
every single time
that I have clutched
one of those paper cones,
filled with chips,
in my hand,
sprinkled on the vinegar
 and blitzed it with salt,
they are absolutely,
no contest,
the best chips in the world.
Proof?

Take a look at those
hundreds of sea gulls
waiting patiently and silently
for one customer
to let a chip slide
out of its paper cup nest
to the beach below.
The wild search for that chip
would scare even a boy scout.
Well, that's my evidence.
Those birds can spot
a tasty chip
from up above the clouds.
They position themselves
in full view of the chip wagon,
that oasis of fast-food dreams.
I fling a whole chip
toward the masses of birds,
sharing a portion
of my treasure
with those perfectly carved
black and white creatures
of water and air.
The attack leaves me
reeling in the dust,
while the warriors
fight over what I hold
in my hand,
in my mouth,
in my memory.

Ah, the power of the perfect chip.
Perhaps I shall spare one more
for the winged flock
that hovers over this grey Great Lake.
But no, I eat the last one.
Those birds understand.
They say nothing.
They know the chip wagon
will outlive me.

Bird Feed

I have head lice.
Who knew?
The teacher phoned my dad.
I am out of school until the lice are gone.
He panicked.
Why? He has no hair.
I knew what to do immediately.
We had been studying history,
specifically, Central Africa.
I found an article on-line
about the yellow-billed oxpecker,
that feeds on the ticks that live
on the hide of the black rhinoceros.
In science talk, the bird is called
Buphagus erythrorhynchus.
These birds live on the backs
of these giant creatures, feasting on bugs.
What has this bird got to do
with head lice, you ask?
Well, my information states that
they are relatives of the starling.
We have starlings in our yard!
I am going to get a blanket,
lay it on the grass,
sit on it with some birdfeed in my hair,
and welcome the birds
to rest and relax on my head.

They then will spot the head bugs
and devour them all.
I can certainly cope with a couple of birds
on my head for an afternoon.
I have my iPad, and
I will read all about these birds,
and write my science report.
If this doesn't get me an A in science,
life isn't fair.

On Guard!

My friend's brother would not give up.
No one could stop him.
Every day at sunrise,
he was glued to the kitchen window,
broom in hand, prepared to battle.
Oh, he loved the birds,
make no mistake about that.
But the squirrels – they were a horse
of a different colour.
They were stealing the birdseed,
lunching on sunflower seeds,
filling their cheeks and bellies
with the only food the birds would have
over the frozen winter.
Those rodents had stolen
acorns and chestnuts
and heaven knows what else.

But the starlings, the chickadees –
their food was gone, and their lives
were at risk.
My friend's brother bought or built
every type of bird feeder
you could imagine –
dishes on poles, boxes covered with net,
bowls that stood on clothes pegs –
and still they came, those nut gatherers,
ready for any situation,
controlling the birds,
the seeds, and my friend's brother.
Finally, he could stand it no longer.
He pitched his tent
out by the bird feeder.
Night and day, he fought
the bushy-tailed thieves.
You've heard of scarecrows.
Well, my friend's brother
was laughed at in the neighbourhood,
wearing his raccoon-tailed hat
and deer-hide jacket.
Personally, I never laughed at him.
After all, he was my friend's brother.
I gladly gave him
all of my family's healthy cereal
to feed his feathered friends.
I trust he would do the same for me
(if I were nuts about birds,
which I'm not, but could be.)

A Bobbin' Robin

The song says that spring arrives
"When the red, red, robin
comes bob, bob, bobbin' along,"
and lo and behold, I see one
on the front lawn and it is indeed
bobbin' along. Looking for worms,
no doubt, those sad creatures
who felt so safe buried
in the still warm earth.
Sorry for the worm,
happy for the warm,
I cheer the robin onward
into spring rain and green grass
and daffodils and tulips and tree buds
and baseball and please please please —
summer.
O harbinger of all things young again,
I salute thy big red belly.

Harbingers of Spring

I am sitting on the back deck
of the farmhouse
owned by Barb and Dale,
on the first warm day
in April when they spy
a woodpecker, while I,
to our left, spot a nuthatch
pecking at the birdfeeder,
as two robins hop along
on the still-soaked grass,
when suddenly a crow,
a great loud crow,
flaps by, scaring the birds
into safer air, so we
step back inside,
knowing the feathered
beings had forced the sun
to warm our souls
in welcomed spring.

Barn Time

"They're back," Shelley called out to Barry.
She had opened the large barn door,
looked up,
and there were the barn swallows,
staring down, nesting in the rafters.
One swooped right across her nose
and without hesitating,
straight out
the small broken window,
welcoming the couple home
after the city winter.

"They are back from where?"
Barry wondered,
"Mexico, Florida, Columbia?"
The birds returned
on cue, every spring, hungry for horse flies,
wasps, moths — two mates, hungry for bugs,
soon ready for a brood of chicks,
content in their mudded grass nests.

Barry took the tarp off Madeleine,
the 1968 Volkswagen Bug
he was restoring in the barn.
The swallows watched, unperturbed,
(who needs wheels?), comfortable alongside
the inhabitants of the summer farm-house
next to the barn,
where the people nests were inside.

Birds and humans, neighbours,
barn swallows safe with the couple
who gave them space,
free of rent, above the car,
sharing the spring awakening,
with memories of other times
when creatures standing in the stalls
were sheltered year-round,
unlike these two arriving couples,
two swallows and two swells,
who left each fall
for warmer climes,
knowing they would
meet up again in barn time.

FEARFUL FEATHERS

In my observations,
and in my life experiences,
I have noticed that there can be sadness
in the bird world. Their lives swoop by,
and danger follows their trails of feathers —
accidents or environmental traps
or natural loss.
Some of my classmates will be afraid
of this section, but poetry goes
where it is needed, and that is my way
of handling the sadness of the cycle
that determines the lives
of these sky creatures.
But to fly high may be its own reward.
Warn them of the dangers, feed them when it is
cold, care for them
when life flutters from their tiny bodies.
Understand the neighbour's cat
and its dreams. Be careful with loud noises when
the bird sleeps.
We must read other poems
about danger and death,
and grasp the rhythm of our days.
Birds are brave, or at least they take life
as it comes,
day by day,
and for me,
poem by poem.

Albatross Wings

Disappear? How could they?
Giant birds with wingspans of ten feet!
They ride the ocean winds,
gliding for hours,
like modern Olympic parasailors,
then float on saltwater, buoyant
and at peace.
Some living for fifty years,
seniors in Birdland.

Do they remember caring for each chick
for almost a year, living in a community
on a remote island, mating for life?
Do they remember?

Look up.
The great birds follow the ship,
waiting for everything we discard — handouts,
the bits and pieces of sea life
that mean nothing to us and life to them.
We weight the fishing lines
so the hooks fall deep into the brine,
far from the feathered hunters.
We toss the garbage at night,
in the darkness.
But still the scavengers swallow
the lines, the bait, the hooks,
the three-pronged hooks,
unknowingly trapping themselves,

ending their lives on the barbs,
until their wings slowly sink
beneath the waves.

We see the albatross behind us.
We shout warnings in the wet air.
Unheard by the birds, we return
to our tasks,
pulling in the lines,
removing the fish,
discarding the dead feathered corpses.

Which birds will follow us when these are extinct?
What shadows will darken our decks,
warning us of death storms?
Is this the way of the world — fish, bird, man?
All caught in the same trap, needy, lost.

Winged-wonders that remind us
of the never-ending circle.

Warning

Could a canary save your life?
Ask a miner working underground
a hundred years ago.
Before entering a mine to begin
slamming a pickaxe at a wall of coal,
his officer carried a small cage
holding a tiny canary.
If that bird swayed on its perch
before falling, a warning
of poisonous fumes could be shouted
to those men in line behind.
O little bird, men lived because of you.
But there were no bird songs
inside the mine.
None.

Silent Fear

Somewhere in the woods
Stands a tree near the stream
Stares an owl in the night
Shines the moon on the rise
Sits a mouse near his hole
Soars the feathers on the wings
Strikes the victim of the night
Sings the cycle of the world
Set inside the silent woods.

Scavengers

The creature lies there by the road,
The cars go by, the drivers stare.
Life seems careless, carcass lifeless,
Only birds seek something there.

Life's great cycle. Birds continue,
Finding nourishment from death.
Pecking, plucking, pulling, stabbing,
The creature giving, minus breath.

The birds are finished, sun is setting,
In one fell swoop they find the sky.
They fly off to their other venues,
Nature's cycle: live and die.

A Force of Nature

When the pigeon flew over our roof
I watched the dip and swirl of his flight path
as he showed us his feathered manoeuvres
and we knew he was ours, our mascot.
Every day, our banded friend appeared
at the curbside, awaiting crumbs of affection.
Then, against the blue he flew as we stared.

The sound that followed was as if a grenade
had exploded. The feathers became a cloud
as the hawk struck the pigeon in midair.
My heart stopped at nature's tough truth.
The pigeon was gone and the hawk
disappeared against the sun.
Grey-white feathers float to the ground.

Was this an abuse of power? Will the weaker
always be vanquished? Hawk as royalty.
Nature's rules unwritten. We are but a part
of it all, hawks and pigeons and us.
Who knew? Who knew?
Family members come and go.
Hawks everywhere.

Breathless Shadows

No one understands the magic
of a bird until it is held in the hand, lifeless.
The neck flops to the side,
and the body is so light, like dust.
"As light as a feather," they say.
Lighter, I say.
When the breath that was the bird
is gone, gravity is no more.
And what will I do
with this wisp of song-making?
How can a hole in the earth
contain something so unearthly,
a sky shadow that fell,
and now rests in my palm.
I shall place it between the V
of the branches of this tree.
They will grow around the feathers,
and one day a bodger
will cut into the wood
and find this tiny fragment
of air and feather,
and bird and tree will be united.

Hope is the Thing with Feathers

Emily Dickinson wrote
"Hope is the thing with feathers."

I know what she meant.
When I see those tiny birds
zooming past the tree
outside my bedroom window,
soaring, diving, landing
for a moment,
(until some hidden signal
sends them off),
I am filled with joy.
Like seeing a rainbow,
or a sunset,
or a crocus,
or a pussy willow.
And a bird lying on the grass
strikes fear in my heart.
No winged thing must die.
Let them fly.
They carry my future.
I believe in all those tiny hearts
living above the trees.
When I die, it will be the birds
that carry my soul
to a waiting spirit
who needs to be born
so that I can go on living.
Do not harm any feathers.

You never know whose bird
will take the journey.
When you hear a baby cry,
one bird has flown
straight and strong.
When you hear the sound
of wings beating,
You will remember hope.

The Broken Wing

It was lying on the steps of our front porch.
The wing was bent awkwardly, no doubt broken.
In the kitchen, I had found a small wicker basket,
and I gingerly picked up the pigeon
and placed it on a towel in the makeshift nest.
I called my grandmother and she came over.
The two of us stared at the bird,
and gently stroked its feathers.
Some pigeons recover with care.
This one did not. That night, it was gone.
My grandmother found a metal cookie box
and we placed the bird, wrapped in the towel,
inside it. I dug the hole in the garden,
and she placed the tiny red coffin in it.
I covered it with earth, and she said,
"From sky to earth to dust."
We walked to the porch and sat for a while.
After she left, I went upstairs to my room
and wrote this poem. I feel better now.

Bluebird

Whooping Cranes

We can count
fifty whooping cranes
in our world.
They are the tallest
of the North American birds,
like white statues,
disappearing
as the wilderness
diminishes,
until now,
when we count those few.

Why do we care?
Are they a symbol
of a spirit that flies–
that can't fight back?
Is it a losing battle
keeping alive a bird
that doesn't even know
what extinct means?

Oil Spill

It was covered in gunk.

A seabird being lifted up

by a scientist

on the TV news

to show the effects

of the oil spill in the ocean.

I want to fly to Alaska

and help these birds.

But I cannot leave my life here.

I stare into the TV screen,

hoping they will be oil-free

and airborne again.

Window Pains

According to the U.S. Fish and Wildlife Service,
"One of the greatest hazards to birds is plate glass,
with windows in homes and offices killing
as many as one billion birds each year."

The woman who picks up
the dead birds
at the base of the office tower
every morning
before the workers arrive
can't identify the species,
their feathered bodies
shattered beyond recognition.
Her cloth sack is filled,
but then she finds a hummingbird,
still breathing,
stunned but not killed
by his own reflection
in Death's window.
Why a hummingbird?
What symbol of life
should we sense?
The woman cradles it
until it stirs, flutters,
and flies into the morning.
The woman carries the sack
inside the back entrance.
The office workers will enter,
unsuspecting.

But they will miss
the hummingbird's miracle,
and the woman's tears.

Dads, Cats and Birds

I begged for a kitten.
My dad ran through all his excuses:
allergies
cost
shots
fleas
food.
(The truth is he hates cats.
I don't know why.)

He said he would look into it.
A big mistake.
I never forgot.

Sixteen months passed and
I again begged for a kitten
reminding him of his promise.

He searched for more reasons
and then by luck,
our neighbour's cat Marble
had chased
a fallen baby robin
into a narrow lane
between our houses
and, too late,
we removed
the dead feathers
from its claws.

I fled to my room
and wept over the loss
of the baby bird's life.
My dad did not know
how to comfort me.

And yet, he bought me
a kitten (an Abyssinian).
I love it, but I love my dad more.
Cats and birds,
Fathers and sons.
We need to forgive them all.

STORY FEATHERS

For a scientist, stories may be
useful bits of information
that may help make sense
of why we all behave as we do.
And watching nature's stories
reveals shadows of our own.
We need to, like the birds, be watchful
of what we can learn
from the tales that confront us all the time.
Stories told, stories old, told in paintings on cave walls,
on bits of leather held in urns,
and for me, all poems are stories:
who wrote them? Why? Why as poems?
Thousands of years in one story of ravens and doves,
of flying dinosaurs, of species lost to us forever.
We live alongside the birds who fly into our dreams
and lay perfect oval futures
filled with stories as yet untold.
And the birds will carry these stories
from county to country, from wooden huts to palaces.
And we will turn them into poems
so that we remember the words, or write them down
with feather pens on parchment,
or keyboard them to fly across the screen.

Feathered Fighters

My father has never been a huge fan
of pigeons. Not many people are I guess.
I don't know why.
Their feathers flash with iridescent
blues and greys, with white baseball caps
sitting on their heads.
They move along the deck like robots
on a mission. And that is the correct term,
mission.
Carrier pigeons who fought in World War II.
Military spies.
Carrying messages across enemy lines.
Codes rolled into a feather glued
to the bird's back. Mini backpacks strapped
onto the pigeon, like a student
heading off to school.
Some feathered operatives
were even awarded medals
at the end of the war.
Like the bird warrior William of Orange
who flew 240 miles in 4 hours,
saving thousands of lives.
And his comrades in flight,
32 other pigeons,
were given the Dickin Medal
for distinguished service to their country.

And that is why I feed this one pigeon
who appears every evening
on our third-floor balcony.
Crumbs, usually.
He may be a descendant of William of Orange,
and he saves me from the loneliness of the city
at dusk. My award winner.

The Bird Artist

"The face of the bird you have drawn
looks like a wooden decoy," she said.
Do we ever want advice, really want it?
She meant no harm. My art teacher.
My "art in the park" class.
I looked at the face of the duck on my page
and it looked like a duck.
They all look the same, right?
And there and then she ran over the grass
and scooped up the smallest duck
and brought it to me. "Look at its face.
So delicate, designed by nature over centuries.
Are the eyes sad? Is it afraid? Are you afraid?
Are you?" I was. I saw patterns and lines
and colours on its face that I had not imagined.
My drawing was empty of life, of breath.
She took the duck back and released it.
With a wave, she was gone. I stared
at the sketch book. I wanted to draw,
to look again, to create something more
than a decoy. I felt that this bird,
this waterfowl, was pulling my vision
through my fingers.
My hand was moving through my eye memory.
I want to be an artist.
I want what I draw to breathe. Help me.

Footprints

I watch the sandpiper walk the beach,
Then running, stopping, a frequent guest.
Finding insects, a quick leave-taking.
Here and there, just footprints left.

The lake's high waves will take the marks,
No ancient fossil will be found,
Sandpipers take just what's needed,
Then choose sky in place of ground.

I sketch the bird tracks on my pad,
I have a feather in my hand,
I save the memory of this creature —
Just footprints found on silver sand.

The Flood

Noah knew his birds.
He stared at the waters
that filled the horizon.
His ark had done its job
for 40 days and 40 nights.
But where was land?
Was there land?
Where was the new beginning?
Birds. They held the answer.

First: Raven.
Meat eater.
Selfish.
Noah stood on the deck
and released Raven.
Finding its wings again,
Raven soared into the sky.
Noah waited three days.
Raven never returned.
Living on the flesh
of the floating corpses,
why would he?

Second:
Dove.
Silent.
Vegetarian.
Noah stood on the deck
and released Dove.

Finding its wings again,
Dove took the breeze
and drifted into the sky.
Noah waited three days,
and Dove returned.
Noah took the tiny olive branch
from Dove's beak.
Land. Land with olive trees.
Home.

It was over. The deluge finished.
Noah knew his creatures.
He knew birds.
Ever after, the dove of peace.
Of hope.
Of beginnings. An olive branch.
We need that branch now.
Let fly the doves!

A Sky of Birds

No one remembers the birds
that could darken the sun,
clouds of flying feathers,
a wind of pigeons,
a century ago. Disappeared today,
nothing left of this fog of creatures.
Millions, even billions,
of passenger pigeons,
slate blue males, females softer in colour,
the flock taking two hours to pass
over a town, frightening the people
into shocked terror, with a roar
louder than a thousand machines,
than the greatest waterfalls, leaving
the terrain below covered
in white excrement, like snow.
"Rejoice," shouted hunters,
"meat for winter." And the birds fell
by the hundreds, the thousands,
victims of the buckshot that could
never miss the game overhead.
You could wave a pole
and knock down dinner.
Men packed the birds
in wooden barrels and
sent them by train
across the continent —
Chicago, New York, Boston.

Revenge for the crops the birds
had devoured. Their nests were burned,
their squabs trampled, their grasses flattened.
Were they struck with disease, with bird flu,
or did they simply die out?
From millions of birds to a genetic leftover
that scientists may use to rebirth the birds.
But never again will there be clouds of them
signalling the end of the world,
covering the sky, filling the air
with the sounds of dozens of steamboats
where there was no river, just woods,
just fields, tree branches laden
with so many pigeons they snapped.
All gone a hundred years ago. In a second,
it seemed. Before ecology awoke,
to save another species.

Birds of Prey

NARRATOR:
Human beings seem to fear most birds of prey.
There are stories of giant birds of prey
snatching up babies and small children, but
these are just tales, don't you agree? Come
and meet four of my friends. They are waiting
for you. There, in the trees.

SCENE 1: OWL

I am owl.
I hunt at night.
Have you met my cousin,
the barn owl?
I have many cousins,
But I would not say we are friends.
Oh, I hear you whispering.
My hearing is sharp.
Pardon me, but I must turn my head
to see you.
My eyes are protected
by a ring of bone.
I notice you wear eye glasses —
I can spot mice, rabbits
in the dark of night.
Pardon me, I need to spit. Arghh!
I see bits of bone and hair
in this pellet.

Look! My eggs are in the nest.
Pure white eggs.
As if they had been carved
from snow.

SCENE 2: EAGLE

I am Bald Eagle.
Do not hide!
I can see in front of me
and at the side — all at once.
I see four times better than you.
Look! See that rabbit one mile away?
Ha! You see nothing!
Of course I can hear.
Not as well as owl,
But I can hear!
I have 700 feathers; you have none.
And I can swim if I have to.
For fish, I love fish.
Last year, I ate dead seal
for two weeks.
Delicious.
Dead or alive, food is food.
I eat what I want.
I have no enemies.
I am Bald Eagle.

SCENE 3: HAWK

I am Hawk.
I hunt in daylight.
I am never afraid.
My uncle is Bald Eagle.
Have you seen him?
I mate for life.
Look! My partner is doing
a cartwheel in the sky.
I shall join him.

Did you see us?
Flying up into the clouds
and diving down together.
We laugh at jet planes!
Wait! I see something moving.
I will return.

Do you see this snake?
Delicious
Want a bite?

SCENE 4: FALCON

I am Falcon.
Be careful of my beak.
It is hooked and sharp.
Oh, and my feet have long, curved claws.
We call them talons.
They help me hold my food while my beak
rips the food apart.
I have to eat, don't you?

My owner thinks he has trained me
I rest on his wrist.
Do I look peaceful?
Remember: I have trained him.

I fly when I want to.
I kill what I choose.
Since his wrist is comfortable.
I like sitting here.
Waiting.
Watching.

Two Birds

"Why are you flying?"
The caged bird was spying.

"Why are you caged?"
Said the free bird, enraged.

"There are dangers outside!"
The caged bird cried.

"But I need the sky!"
The free bird flew high.

"What will you drink?"
"Rivers, I think."

"Whom will you love?"
"A bird from above."

"And who will love you?"
"My keeper will do."

"My fate is to roam."
"My cage is my home."

Two birds sing a song,
But one is now gone.

Give Thanks for the Birds

Look. Twelve noon. The church bell chimes.
She is on the bench in the park. Always
at noon. Feeding the pigeons. Breadcrumbs.
The same coat, long and brown. A hat that
covers her hair. Boots like my mother wore
40 years ago. Gloves without fingers. Brown.
The pigeons surround her, know her, hungry.
She showers the air with bread crumbs,
and speak-laughs, "Plenty for all of you!"
The paper bag's contents seem endless,
as her hand dips in and out, the birds
hustling and bustling, no one shoving or
stealing from each other. A flock of friends
fed by Mary Magdalene, every day, in lieu
of sons and daughters, or sisters growing
old together, or a partner to warm her hands
when all is done. Maybe the pigeons are
enough, nature's reward for her generosity
of spirit, filling each day with purpose, intent.
I will share my chocolate bar at lunch with friends,
a feeble attempt at touching her spirit and hoping
there will at least be pigeons when I am old.

The Incredible Shrinking Dinosaurs

Who could have known that
the origin of flying feathers
would be discovered inside
ancient rocks, fossils, buried
with secrets revealed only
by archeologists searching
for dinosaurs, and discovering
bird connections to those
giant creatures from movies
that we have come to love.
Maniraptoran theropods
weighing 500 pounds
laid eggs as birds do.
Some creatures covered
with plumage. Dinosaur feathers!
Such a diversity of dinobirds.
Many with long bony tails.
Skulls that shrank
into bird-sized heads.
Not all happened at once.
Millions and millions of years
to become birds, minor alterations
as the creatures evolved,
different species of warm-blooded flying
feathers, smaller and smaller
through all those years, until today
when the monsters
are gone, destroyed by missiles

from the sky, and we find
these beaked descendants
hovering over our past dreams
of Jurassic Park,
knowing what we do not,
twittering and screaming
their history,
strutting and soaring,
fuelled by memories
of the giant shadows
that once owned the earth.

Bird Brains

I read about Serenity Park
In the New York Times.
A sanctuary for abandoned
and injured parrots
at the Veteran's Medical Centre,
where ex-military men and women,
damaged from their time in battle,
victims of PTSD, find empathy
by bonding with one bird
for mutual healing.

Like these men and women warriors,
parrots are social beings who,
in the absence of their species,
find community with humans,
learning to speak the language
of those outside their cages,
who are imprisoned by their own lost lives.
Two creatures supporting each other,
both desperate to connect, bird and human.

One parrot is cleaning the nails of a soldier.
Another is flossing a soldier's teeth.
Sitting on their heads, or in a shirt pocket,
resting on a shoulder, chattering words
from previous owners, in different languages
and dialects, these rescued birds,
with an alien intelligence, rescue others.

I want to fly to L.A.
I want to find Serenity Park.
I am not a soldier.
I have wounds.
I need to love a parrot.
Will he love me back?

Kevin's Project

I sit beside Kevin in our English class.
He is quiet, like me.
I found out that he is a First Nations son,
and lives in our city just around the corner
from me. His project was so interesting compared
to mine. It changed my thoughts on birds forever.
He wrote about his Peoples' Bird Legends,
with black and white illustrations
that were symbols:

- because the crow had the power of talk,
  it had wisdom for others to learn from;
- because the eagle was sacred and clever,
  it was messenger to the Creator;
- because the hawk could fight while flying,
  it protected all from the evil spirits
  that fill the air;
- because the hummingbird lives with a partner,
  it was a symbol of devotion and eternity;
- because of its strength, raven sensed
  that danger had passed and good luck will follow;
- because owls could see beyond the grave,
  they signified a bad omen.

These were his stories of why his people respect birds.
I believe they are true.

And I read that the geese come
every spring and fall
to feed the First Nations Peoples
on the coast of Hudson's Bay,
and I understand why they are hunted
by the hungry.
Nature follows a cycle, and birds
are the emissaries and martyrs,
and Kevin knows this.

I am no longer ashamed of the turkey
at Thanksgiving; I honor our tradition.
I will invite Kevin to have dinner with us.
He has so much to share. So much.

The Birds' Respond

Birding Rules

We like birders best; anyone can be a birdwatcher.
But birders work at understanding who we really are.

There are billions of you. And billions of us.

We allow birding if the birders are serious. We do not
mind being stared at, but we do not appreciate intruders.

We cannot read words, but others tell us that signs
on some land may say do not trespass. But we are
allowed; we do not leave trash behind, and our droppings
are biodegradable.

Do not come too close to us. Some of us are fragile
and we flee from disturbance.

Birthing is a holy time for us as parents. Stay far away
from our nesting places.

Some of us are homeless in urban centres. We enjoy our
freedom. But we appreciate the tiniest of donated crumbs.

Some of us are show-offs, with colours that shock your
eyes. Others of us are soft grey, pale dusk, shades of sand.
Remember: we all enjoy your stares. At times.

Leave us be. There are laws. We are not to be trained pets.
Only parrots enjoy the safety of cages. They speak your
language.

124

We, too, have our own language. Listen to us.
At dawn. At dusk. Messages carried through the air,
like pollen and perfume. Of love. Fear. Food.

Some pairs stay together for life. Others are tempted
to move on. Why does this concern you? We ignore
your relationships. Do the same for us.

Many of you count our numbers — a bird census — at
Christmas. How many were seen in the marshes, the
woods, the plains, the seaside. Quite inaccurate. Wind, sea,
sun, rain, all affect our travels. Count away if you like.
I myself am hiding in the fir tree. You missed me.

Share these rules with hunters; we remain unarmed.
Let us fly.

The Final Monday:

Feather Poems

My 9th Grade English Project

By Wally Karr, the Bird Guy

For my science teacher, Mr. Moore.

These are my poem feathers,
on the whitest of pages,
like the tracks of a pigeon
on the cleanest city snow.
Each bird is a poem,
and each poem a bird.
Their habitat, food, flight,
and dangers fill my dreams
and visions. My project
has become my world.
Welcome.

The Teacher Responds

You have completed your writing project with flying colours, pun intended. From a weak beginning, you have moved your research and writing into a truly integrated year-end report. Few chose poetry as the form of their writing; no one else chose "birds" as their subject for their composing.

This is an observational writing report, and tells us that as writers, we need to remember the connected qualities of our topics being described and interpreted, but more important, you have shared your thoughts and feelings as a poet. In truth, you have studied yourself as well as the birds. You fly with them. Science, poetry and memoir, all integrated. We all must find our passion.

Your grade is A, and to respect your choices of study, I have written my thoughts about your topic. They follow this assessment. You see, English teachers have feelings, too.

All the best,

W. H. Moore

Remember Emily says that
"hope is the thing with feathers..."

1. They turn the most manicured garden into a wild place, untamed.

2. They mark the passage of seasons, knowing the sun intimately.

3. They feed the earth with nutrients, recycling nature.

4. They kiss plants and create flowered offspring.

5. They help us sing poems and paint skies.

6. They awaken sleeping souls to the natural world.

7. They are ubiquitous, and always.

8. They allow us to consider the heavens and angels.

9. They understand a sense of place, wherever.

10. They need no passports and travel forever.

11. They colour our world with hues unmatched.

12. They teach us that gravity is not all powerful.

13. They fill us with wonder. They simply are.

129

Winged Creatures in the Poems

Albatross
American Woodcock
Bald Eagle
Barn Swallow
Blue Jay
Budgie
Canary
Cardinal
Chickadee
Chicken/Turkey
Crane
Crow
Cuckoo
Dove
Duck
Eagle
Falcon
Fireflies
Flamingo
Geese
Golden-crowned Kinglet
Great Blue Heron
Grey Jay
Hawk
Homing Pigeon
Hummingbird
Loon
Magpie
Mockingbird

Northern Flicker
Nuthatch
Oriole
Ostrich
Ovenbird
Owl
Parakeet
Parrot
Northern Saw-whet Owl
Passenger Pigeon
Pigeon
Raven
Red-breasted Nuthatch
Red-Winged Blackbird
Robin
Rose-breasted Grosbeak
Ruby-throated Hummingbird
Sandpiper
Sea Bird
Seagull
Snow Bunting
Songbird
Sparrow
Starling
Swan
Vulture
Warbler
White-throated Sparrow
Whooping Crane
Woodpecker
Wren

About the authors and illustrator

David Booth is the author of several textbooks for teachers, dozens of anthologies for schools, and many award-winning picture books. He is a well-known international speaker, and a strong advocate for using the best books for young people in home and at school.

Maya Ishiura, illustrator, is a professional artist and set decorator and designer on several popular television shows. She was trained at the National Theatre School in Montreal, and now works in Toronto.

Wally Karr is a virtual student in a grade 7, 8 and 9 Junior High. He enjoys school, especially English, and is on the track team. His nickname is Bird Guy. He lives with his father and grandmother. His best friends are Mara and E. J.

William H. Moore was a Grade 7, 8 and 9 English teacher. Born in England, he is an authority on poetry, both classic and contemporary. He is considered an excellent teacher and a leader in education.

Made in the USA
Middletown, DE
24 August 2018